MW01609959

Copyright 2019 @ Alex Smith

All rights reserved.

No part of this book may be reproduced,
stored in a retrieval system or transmitted
in any form or by any means, electronic,
photocopying, recording or othewise,
without written permission of the author.

This book is a work of fiction. Any
resemblance to actual persons, living or dead,
business, events or locales is entirely
coincidental.

Did you hear about the new movie "Constipation"?

It hasn't come out yet.

Yesterday I accidentally swallowed some food coloring.

The doctor says I'm ok, but I feel like I've dyed a little inside.

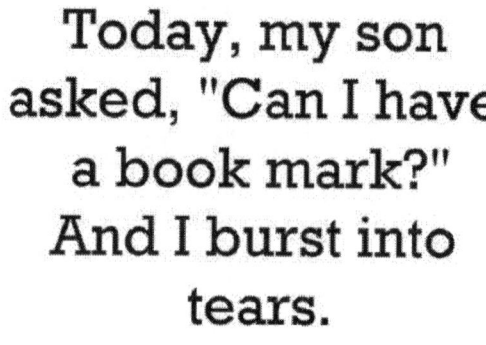

Today, my son asked, "Can I have a book mark?" And I burst into tears.

11 years old and he still doesn't know my name is Brian.

What did 2 say to 3 when they saw 6 act like an idiot?
Don't mind him. He's just a product of our times.

I went to an antenna wedding.

The ceremony was boring as hell, but the reception was great!

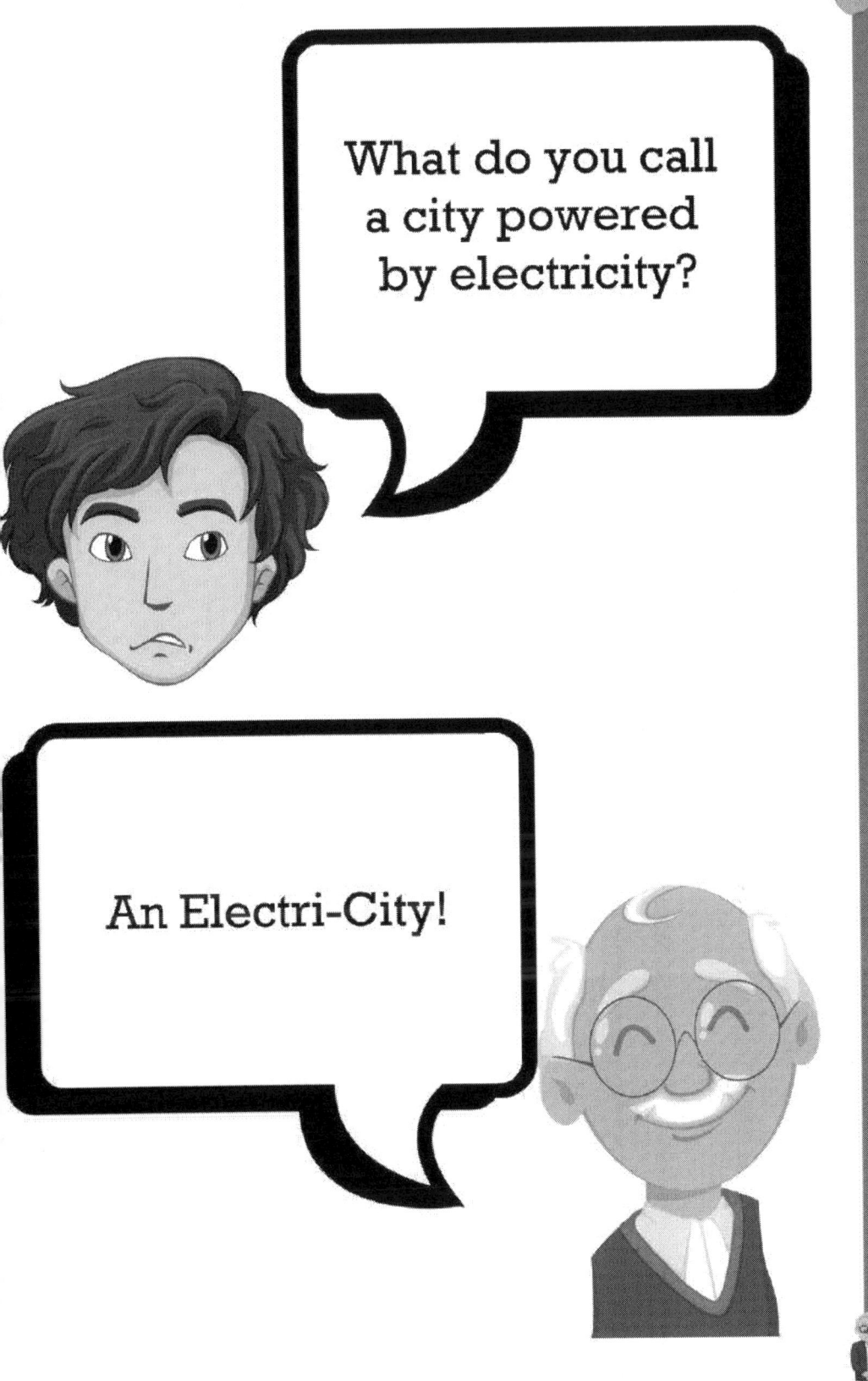

What happens when a frog's car dies?

He needs a jump. If that doesn't work he has to get it toad.

Why are the North Koreans the best at geometry?

Because they've got a Supreme Ruler.

What rhymes with boo and stinks?

You!

What's the slipperiest country?

Greece.

Last night me and my wife watched three movies back to back.

Luckily I was the one facing the TV.

What's an astronaut's favorite part of a computer?

The space bar.

What do you call a guy with a rubber toe?

Roberto!

This graveyard looks overcrowded.

People must be dying to get in there.

What is the best way to communicate with a fish?

Drop it a line.

How many South Americans does it take to change a light bulb?

A Brazilian.

Me: "Dad, make me a sandwich!"

Dad: "Poof, You're a sandwich!"

How do lawyers say goodbye?

We'll be suing ya!

Why is Peter Pan always flying?

He neverlands!

What do snowmen call their offspring?

Chill-Dren.

Why can't the bank keep a secret?

It has too many tellers.

What do you call an elephant that doesn't matter?

An irrelephant.

What do you call a snowman with a six pack?

An abdominal snowman.

Why are doctors always calm?

Because they have a lot of patients.

What did the bra say to the hat?

You go on a head, I gotta give these two a lift.

I'm thinking about removing my spine.

I feel like it's only holding me back.

Did you hear about the circus fire?

It was in tents.

The difference between a numerator and a denominator is a short line.

Only a fraction of people will understand this!

What do you call someone who is afraid of Santa?

A clausterphobic.

Why don't oysters share their pearls?

Because they're shellfish.

What brand of car does an Egg drive?

A Yolkswagen.

I just watched a program about beavers.

It was the best dam program I've ever seen.

Why are spiders so smart?

They can find everything on the web.

When the grocery store clerk asks me if I want the milk in a bag, I always tell him,

"No, I'd rather drink it out of the carton!"

What is a Christmas tree's favorite candy?

Ornamints.

The recipe said, "Set the oven to 180 degrees."

But now I can't open it because the door faces the wall.

Who invented King Arthur's round table?

Sir Cumference!

The secret service isn't allowed to yell "Get down!" anymore when the president is about to be attacked.

Now they have to yell "Donald, Duck!"

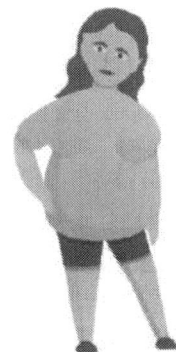

Why was the Thanksgiving dinner so expensive?

It Had 24 Carrots.

What's the difference between a poorly dressed man on a tricycle and a well-dressed man on a bicycle?

Attire.

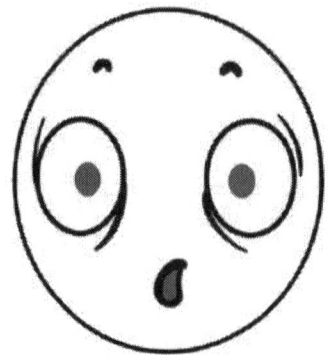

A policy officer caught two kids playing with a firework and a car battery.

He charged one and let the other off.

What did the fried rice say to the shrimp?

Don't wok away from me.

How do moths swim?

Using the butterfly stroke.

I would avoid the sushi if I was you.

It's a little fishy!

Can a turkey jump higher than the Empire State Building?

Yes, of course! A building can't jump at all.

What did the drummer name his twin daughters?

Anna 1, Anna 2!

A red and blue ship have collided in the Caribbean sea.

Apparently the survivors are marooned.

How does a penguin build it's house?

Igloos it together.

Why is there a donut sitting at the dentist's office?

It's there to get a filling.

Regular naps prevent old age,

especially if you take them while driving.

What does a baby computer call his father?

Data.

I saw a robbery at an Apple Store.

Does that make me an iWitness?!

What do you call a turkey on the day after thanksgiving?

Lucky.

I tried to catch some fog.

But I mist.

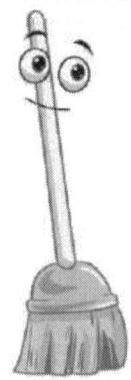

There's a new type of broom in stores.

It's sweeping the nation!

Why did the coffee file a police report?

It got mugged.

Why do fish make such lousy tennis players?

They're afraid of coming close to the net.

Standing in a park, I was wondering why a Frisbee gets larger the closer it gets.

Then it hit me.

What did the fisherman say to the magician?

Pick a cod, any cod.

My uncle named his dogs Rolex and Timex.

They're his watch dogs!

A lady was picking through the frozen turkeys at the grocery store for Thanksgiving day, but couldn't find one big enough for her family.

She asked a stock boy, "do these turkeys get any bigger?"

"No, ma'am. They're dead."

Why should you wear 2 pants when you golf?

In case you get a hole-in-one.

What time did the man go to the dentist?

Tooth hurty!

Are insecticides good for mosquitos?

"Not at all, it kills them!"

There's a fine line between fishing....

and standing on the shore looking like an idiot.

I like to keep my money in the freezer.

That way I always have cold, hard cash.

Why did the coach go to the bank?

To get his quarter back.

So a vowel saves another vowel's life.

The other vowel says, "Aye E! I owe you!"

What always comes at the end of Thanksgiving?

The letter G.

How well did I hang up that picture?

I nailed it.

Can I watch TV?

Yes but don't turn it on.

When does a joke become a dad joke?

When it becomes apparent!

I read the other day that people eat more bananas than monkeys.

No surprises there. I can't even remember the last time I ate a monkey.

If you take away the looks, money, intelligence, charm and success -

there's no real difference between me and George Clooney.

Did you hear about the man who fell into an upholstery machine?

He's fully recovered.

I told my girlfriend she drew her eyebrows too high.

She seemed surprised!

What was the turkey suspected of?

Fowl play.

What do you get when you cross a snowman and a vampire?

Frost bite.

What did the late tomato say to the other tomatoes?

Don't worry I'll ketchup.

My wife is really mad at the fact that I have no sense of direction.

So I packed up my stuff and right!

My wife dared doubt my craftsmanship when I was changing the light switch.

Ha Ha, she's in for a shock.

I won $3 million on the lottery this weekend, so I decided to donate a quarter of it to charity.

Now I have $2,999,999.75.

What do you call it when Batman skips church?

Christian Bale.

My wife told me I had to stop acting like a flamingo.

So I had to put my foot down!

Why do crabs never give to charity?

Because they're shellfish.

Where is the first math problem mentioned in the Bible?

When God told Adam and Eve to go forth and multiply.

What did the mama turkey say to her naughty son?

If your papa could see you now, he'd turn over in his gravy.

What is the best Christmas present ever?

A broken drum – you can't beat it!

"Dad, I'm going to take a bath."

"I think the tub is too heavy for you to take."

I dreamt about drowning in an ocean made of orange soda last night.

It took me a while to work out it was just a Fanta Sea.

I used to work in a shoe recycling shop.

It was sole destroying.

What is red and flies through the air?

A tomato in a helicopter.

Want to hear a joke about construction?

I'm still working on it.

What's Forrest Gump's Facebook password?

1forest1.

My friend says to me, "What rhymes with orange?"

And I told him, "No it doesn't!"

What did Al Gore play on his guitar?

Algorithm.

What do you call a cow during an earthquake?

A milkshake.

A dung beetle walks into a bar and asks:

"Is this stool taken?"

How do we know Peter was a rich fisherman?

By his net income.

What did the buffalo say when his son left for school?

Bison!

What do you call a fly without wings?

A walk.

A furniture store keeps calling me.

All I wanted was one night stand.

They are testing a revolutionary new blender.

But they're getting mixed results.

My boss asked me who is the stupid one, me or him?

I told him everyone knows he doesn't hire stupid people.

To whoever stole my copy of Microsoft Office, I will find you.

You have my Word!

Spring is here!

I got so excited I wet my plants!

What do Alexander The Great and Winnie The Pooh have in common?

Same middle name.

What did one eye say to the other eye?

Between you and me, something smells.

Why couldn't the shellfish farmer go for a run?

He pulled a mussel.

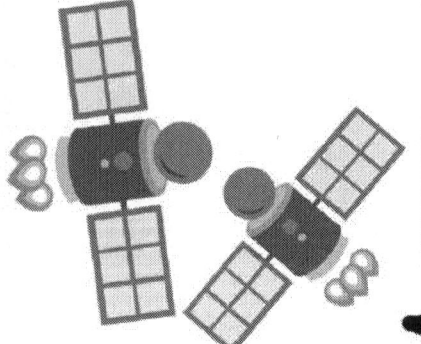

Two satellites got married,

the ceremony wasn't much but the reception was great.

Did you hear about the girl who quit her job at the doughnut factory?

She was fed up with the hole business.

If a child refuses to sleep during nap time,

are they guilty of resisting a rest?

"What is a bunny without a carrot?"

"Hungry!"

I'm great at multitasking.

I can waste time, be unproductive and procrastinate all at once.

My boss asked me to do some odd jobs.

He gave me a list of ten, so I only did 1,3,5,7 and 9.

I'm so good at sleeping.

I can do it with my eyes closed!

Why aren't koalas actual bears?

They don't meet the koalafications.

How do trees access the internet?

They log in.

DAD: I was just listening to the radio on my way in to town, apparently an actress just killed herself.

MOM: Oh my! Who!?

DAD: Uh, I can't remember... I think her name was Reese something?
MOM: WITHERSPOON!!!!!????
DAD: No, it was with a knife...

Two goldfish are in a tank. One says to the other,

"do you know how to drive this thing?"

Why didn't Noah go fishing?

He only had two worms.

What do you call a can opener that doesn't work?

A can't opener.

I wasn't going to get a brain transplant.

But then I changed my mind.

What did the caretaker say when they jumped out of the store cupboard?

"Supplies!"

My boss told me to have a good day.

So I went home!

What did the mother molecule say to the child molecule?

I've got my ion you!

What word is always spelled wrong in the dictionary?

Wrong.

What do you call a man with a rubber toe?

Roberto.

I bought some shoes from a drug dealer.

I don't know what he laced them with, but I was tripping all day!

Did Eve ever have a date with Adam?

No, just an apple.

Did you know the first French fries weren't actually cooked in France?

They were cooked in Greece.

Why Davids should never loose their ID?

Because then you have to call them Davs.

Why did the invisible man turn down the job offer?

He couldn't see himself doing it!

What do you do with a dead chemist?

Barium.

Dad, can you put the cat out?

I didn't know it was on fire.

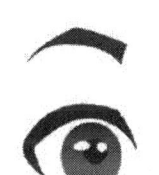

What do you call someone with no body and no nose?

Nobody knows.

Why are there so many elderly people in Church?

They're cramming for the final.

What did George Washington say to his men before crossing the Delaware?

"Get in the boat."

Why can't you have a nose that is 12 inches long?

Because then it would be a foot.

England doesn't have a kidney bank.

But it does have a Liverpool.

What do you call a fish with two knees?

A two-knee fish!

Did you know that UPS and Fedex are going into a merger?

They will be called Fed-Ups now.

What do you call a factory that sells passable products?

A satisfactory!

What did the chemist say when he found two new isotopes of Helium?

HeHe.

What do sea monsters eat for lunch?

Fish and ships.

WAITRESS: "Soup or salad?"

DAD: "I don't want a SUPER salad, I want a regular salad."

What do you call a fat psychic?

A four-chin teller.

My daughter screeched, "Daaaaad, you haven't listened to one word I've said, have you!?"

What a strange way to start a conversation with me...

What kind of man was Boaz before he married Ruth?

Ruthless.

I got fired at my job at the bank today.

Someone asked me to check their balance so I pushed them over.

Have you ever tried to eat a clock?

It's very time consuming.

To the man in the wheelchair that stole my camouflage jacket...

You can hide but you can't run.

I love my rock-hard, honed six-pack so much that...

I protect it with a good layer of lard.

Why did the old man fall in the well?

Because he couldn't see that well!

You know, people say they pick their nose,

but I feel like I was just born with mine.

What do we have that Adam never had?

Ancestors.

I'm not calling her a gold digger,

but she did move to California in 1849.

What is the difference between an angry circus owner and a Roman barber?

One is a raving showman, the other is a shaving roman.

Can one bird make a pun?

No, but toucan.

Why did the cookie cry?

Because his father was a wafer so long!

The fattest knight at King Arthur's round table was Sir Cumference.

He acquired his size from too much pi.

How does Moses make his coffee?

Hebrews it.

I stayed up all night wondering where the sun went.

Then it dawned on me.

I wanted to go on a diet,

but I feel like I have way too much on my plate right now.

Cannibals aren't very sociable.

They're all fed up with people.

Why don't skeletons ever go trick or treating?

Because they have no body to go with!

What do you call a man who spent all summer at the beach?

A tangent.

I got so angry the other day...

when I couldn't find my stress ball.

How can you tell if a ant is a boy or a girl?

They're all girls, otherwise they'd be uncles.

Mom: "How do I look?"

Dad: "With your eyes."

Why can't you hear a pterodactyl go to the bathroom?

Because the pee is silent.

3 unwritten rules of life...

1.
2.
3.

What did Adam and Eve do after they were kicked out of the Garden of Eden?

They raised a little Cain.

Did you hear about the giant that threw up?

It's all over the town!

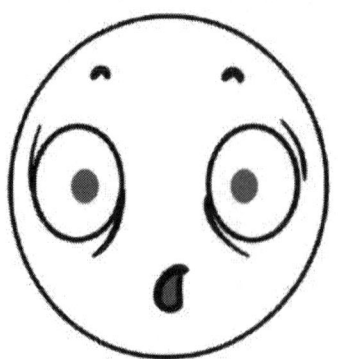

I remember the first time I saw a universal remote control.

I thought to myself: "well this changes everything".

Did you hear about the chameleon who couldn't change color?

He had a reptile dysfunction.

I don't know why people have a problem with wigs.

It's a look anybody can pull off!

Why was the toilet paper rolling down the hill?

It was in a rush to get to the bottom.

What do you call the heavy breathing someone makes while trying to hold a yoga pose?

Yoga pants.

What has two butts and kills people?

An assassin.

Why did God create man before woman?

Because He didn't want any advice on how to do it.

How do you make holy water?

Freeze it into ice, then drill in some holes.

If Snoop Dogg dies before pot becomes legal in the US,

he will be rolling in his grave.

Did you hear about the guy who had his left side cut off?

He's all right now!

What do you call a man with no arms and no legs lying in front of your door?

Matt.

When I ask my dad if he's alright,

he replies, "No, I'm half left."

What did the judge say when the skunk walked into the courtroom?

Odor in the Court.

Slept like a log last night ...

woke up in the fireplace.

Made in the USA
Middletown, DE
07 December 2020